RESPIRATORY PHARMACOLOGY

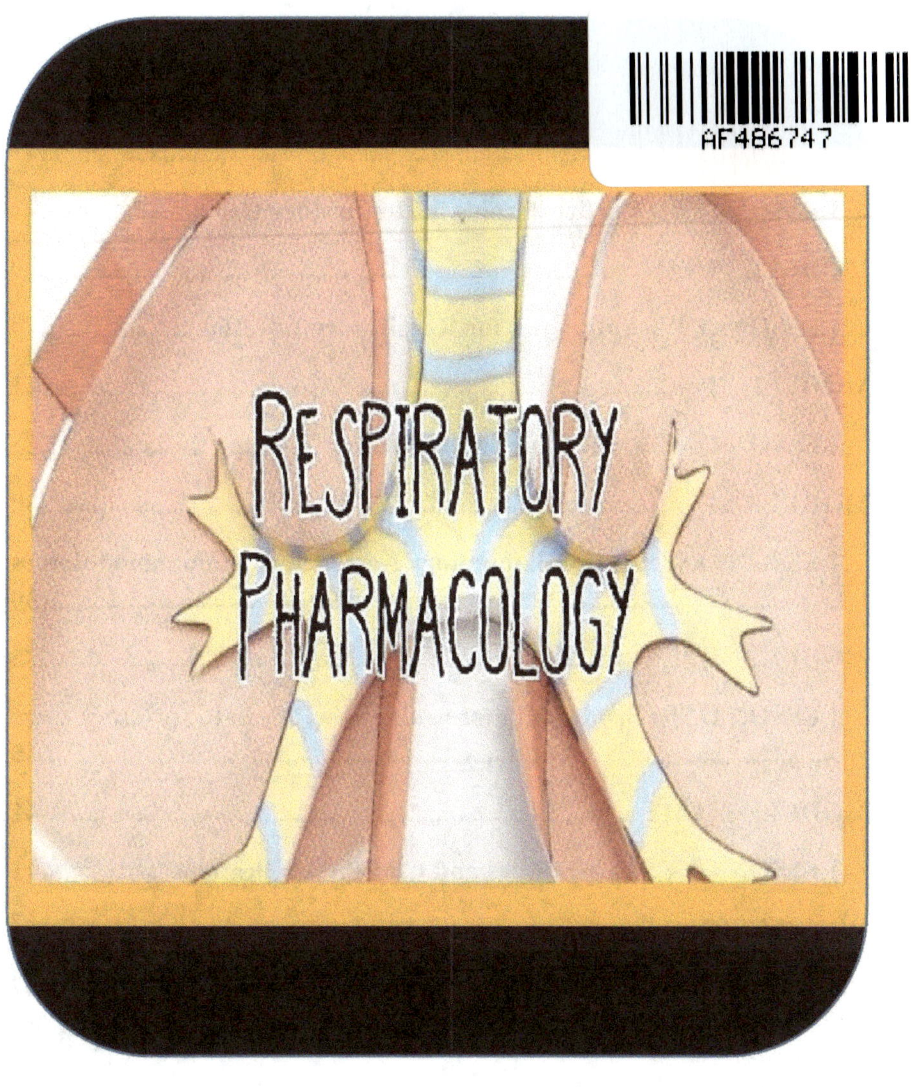

TABLE OF CONTENTS

COURSE OVERVIEW

This comprehensive course on Respiratory Pharmacology is designed for healthcare providers who seek to enhance their understanding and expertise in the management of respiratory conditions. The course delves into the pharmacological principles, therapeutic applications, and clinical considerations of medications used in respiratory care, including bronchodilators, corticosteroids, antibiotics, mucolytics, expectorants, anti-inflammatory agents, and immunomodulators. Through detailed lectures, case studies, and interactive discussions, participants will gain the knowledge necessary to effectively prescribe and manage respiratory medications, improving patient outcomes and quality of life.

COURSE OBJECTIVES

By the end of this course, participants will be able to Understand the Anatomy and Physiology of the Respiratory System, Classify and Describe Respiratory Medications, Apply Pharmacological Principles in Clinical Practice, Evaluate and Monitor Treatment Efficacy and Safety, Educate Patients on Respiratory Medications Incorporate Evidence-Based Practices, Analyze Case Studies to Enhance Clinical Skills, Explore Future Directions in Respiratory Pharmacology. This course aims to equip healthcare providers with a robust understanding of respiratory pharmacology, enabling them to deliver high-quality care and optimize treatment outcomes for patients.

COURSE MATERIALS

To learn this course, **healthcare providers/ participants** must be provided with materials like a Pen, pencil, notebook, and notepad to better understand and make it easy for them to learn.

INTRODUCTION

In the complex and ever-evolving field of healthcare, understanding the intricacies of respiratory pharmacology is crucial for any healthcare provider. Respiratory conditions are among the most common ailments encountered in clinical practice, ranging from acute infections to chronic diseases like asthma and chronic obstructive pulmonary disease (COPD). The effective management of these conditions often hinges on the appropriate use of pharmacological agents. "Mastering Respiratory Pharmacology: A Comprehensive Guide for Healthcare Providers" is designed to be an indispensable resource for those seeking to deepen their knowledge and enhance their clinical skills in this vital area.

Respiratory pharmacology encompasses a wide array of medications, each with its unique mechanisms of action, therapeutic benefits, and potential side effects. This book aims to provide a thorough understanding of these medications, from the commonly used bronchodilators and corticosteroids to the critical role of antibiotics in treating respiratory infections. We will explore how these drugs work at a molecular level, their clinical applications, and the best practices for their administration.

MODULE ONE

LESSON ONE: RESPIRATORY PHARMACOLOGY

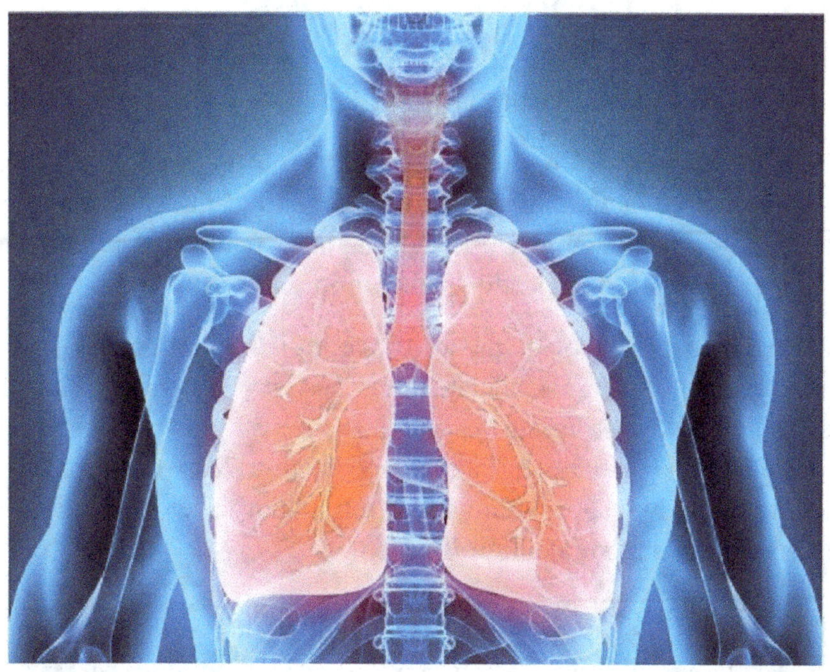

Respiratory pharmacology is a critical field within healthcare, focusing on the medications used to treat various respiratory conditions. These conditions range from acute illnesses like pneumonia and bronchitis to chronic diseases such as asthma, chronic obstructive pulmonary disease (COPD), and interstitial lung diseases. Understanding the pharmacological interventions available for these conditions is essential for healthcare providers to ensure effective and safe patient care.

Historical Context and Evolution

The field of respiratory pharmacology has evolved significantly over the past century. Early treatments for respiratory conditions needed to be more extensive and often ineffective. The advent of modern pharmacology in the mid-20th century brought about a revolution in the treatment of respiratory diseases. The development of bronchodilators and corticosteroids, for example, transformed the management of asthma and COPD, drastically improving patient outcomes and quality of life.

Basic Principles of Respiratory Pharmacology

Respiratory pharmacology is built on the principles of pharmacodynamics and pharmacokinetics.

Pharmacodynamics refers to drugs' effects on the body, including mechanisms of action at the molecular and cellular levels. For instance, bronchodilators work by relaxing smooth muscles in the airways, thus improving airflow in conditions like asthma and COPD.

Pharmacokinetics involves the absorption, distribution, metabolism, and excretion of drugs. Understanding these processes is crucial for determining the appropriate dosage and administration route for each medication. For example, inhaled medications can deliver drugs directly to the lungs, providing rapid relief with fewer systemic side effects compared to oral administration.

Key Drug Classes in Respiratory Pharmacology

Several classes of drugs are commonly used in respiratory care:

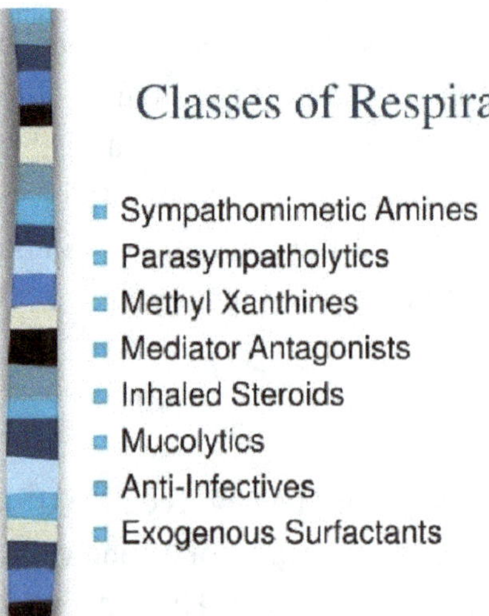

- **Bronchodilators:** These include beta-agonists, anticholinergics, and methylxanthines. They are primarily used to relieve bronchoconstriction in asthma and COPD.
- **Corticosteroids:** Used for their anti-inflammatory properties, corticosteroids can be administered systemically or inhaled. They are a cornerstone in the long-term management of asthma and COPD.
- **Antibiotics:** Critical in treating bacterial infections that can complicate respiratory conditions, such as pneumonia.
- **Antihistamines and Leukotriene Modifiers** are used primarily to reduce inflammation and allergic responses in allergic respiratory conditions and asthma.
- **Mucolytics and Expectorants:** These drugs help thin and clear mucus from the airways, which is beneficial in conditions like chronic bronchitis and cystic fibrosis.

Mechanisms of Action

Understanding the mechanisms of action of respiratory drugs is essential for effective treatment.

- Beta-agonists, such as albuterol, stimulate beta-2 adrenergic receptors in the lungs, leading to bronchodilation.
- Anticholinergics, like ipratropium, block muscarinic receptors, reducing bronchoconstriction and mucus secretion.
- Corticosteroids work by inhibiting inflammatory pathways, reducing swelling and mucus production in the airways.
- Antibiotics target specific bacterial pathogens, disrupting their cellular processes and leading to bacterial death.

Administration Routes

The route of administration can significantly impact the efficacy and safety of respiratory medications.

- Inhalation is the most common route, delivering drugs directly to the lungs, which allows for rapid onset of action and minimal systemic exposure.

- Oral and intravenous routes are used for systemic effects or when inhalation is not feasible.

Importance of Proper Administration Techniques

Proper administration techniques are vital for maximizing the therapeutic benefits of respiratory drugs and minimizing side effects. For instance, using inhalers correctly ensures that the medication reaches the lungs effectively. Training patients on proper inhaler techniques and ensuring adherence to prescribed treatments are critical components of respiratory care.

DISCUSSION QUESTIONS

- How do the anatomy and physiology of the respiratory system influence the pharmacokinetics and pharmacodynamics of respiratory medications?
- What are the key differences in drug delivery methods for respiratory medications, and how do these affect their efficacy and patient adherence?

MODULE TWO

LESSON ONE: BRONCHODILATORS; MECHANISMS AND APPLICATIONS

Bronchodilators are a cornerstone in the treatment of obstructive airway diseases, including asthma and chronic obstructive pulmonary disease (COPD). These medications work

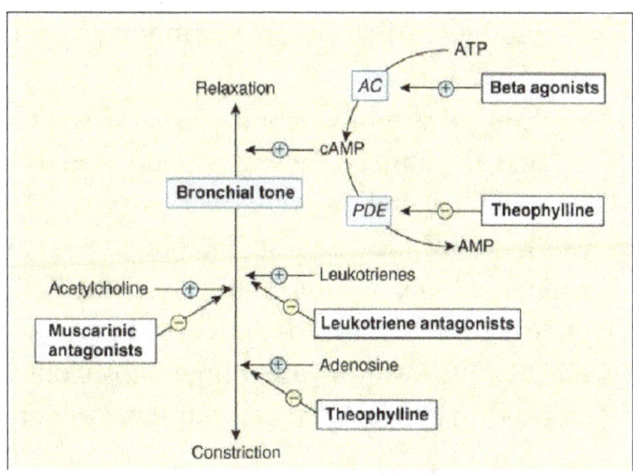

by relaxing the smooth muscles of the airways, thereby improving airflow and alleviating symptoms such as wheezing, shortness of breath, and chest tightness. In this lesson, we will explore the various types of bronchodilators, their mechanisms of action, clinical applications, and administration techniques.

Types of Bronchodilators

Bronchodilators can be broadly categorized into three main types: beta-agonists, anticholinergics, and methylxanthines.

1. **Beta-Agonists:** These are the most commonly used bronchodilators and can be further divided into short-acting beta-agonists (SABAs) and long-acting beta-agonists (LABAs).
   - **Short-Acting Beta-Agonists (SABAs):** Examples include albuterol and levalbuterol. These medications provide quick relief of acute bronchospasm and are often used as rescue inhalers.
   - **Long-Acting Beta-Agonists (LABAs):** Examples include salmeterol and formoterol. These drugs are used for long-term

control and maintenance therapy in asthma and COPD. They are not suitable for acute relief.

2. **Anticholinergics:** These medications block the action of acetylcholine on muscarinic receptors in the airways, leading to bronchodilation.

   - **Short-Acting Anticholinergics:** An example is ipratropium bromide, often used in combination with SABAs for acute exacerbations.
   - **Long-Acting Anticholinergics:** Examples include tiotropium and aclidinium. These drugs are used for maintenance therapy in COPD and, in some cases, asthma.

3. **Methylxanthines:** These include drugs like theophylline and aminophylline. Methylxanthines are less commonly used due to their narrow therapeutic index and potential for significant side effects. They work by inhibiting phosphodiesterase, leading to an increase in cyclic AMP and subsequent bronchodilation.

Mechanisms of Action

Each class of bronchodilators operates through distinct mechanisms to achieve the common goal of airway relaxation.

- **Beta-Agonists:** These drugs stimulate beta-2 adrenergic receptors on the smooth muscle cells of the airways. This stimulation activates adenylate cyclase, increasing the levels of cyclic AMP. Elevated cyclic AMP levels lead to the relaxation of bronchial smooth muscle and bronchodilation.
- **Anticholinergics:** These medications block muscarinic receptors in the airways, preventing the action of acetylcholine, a neurotransmitter that causes bronchoconstriction and mucus secretion. By inhibiting this pathway, anticholinergics promote airway relaxation and reduce mucus production.
- **Methylxanthines:** Theophylline and related drugs inhibit phosphodiesterase, an enzyme that breaks down cyclic AMP. By preventing the degradation of cyclic AMP, methylxanthines promote sustained bronchodilation.

Additionally, they have mild anti-inflammatory effects and can enhance diaphragmatic contractility, aiding respiratory effort.

Clinical Applications

Bronchodilators are used in various clinical scenarios, tailored to the patient's needs and the specific characteristics of the respiratory condition.

1. **Asthma**
   - SABAs are used for quick relief of acute asthma symptoms and exacerbations.
   - LABAs are used in combination with inhaled corticosteroids (ICS) for long-term control and prevention of symptoms. They should not be used as monotherapy due to the risk of severe asthma exacerbations.
2. **Chronic Obstructive Pulmonary Disease (COPD)**
   - SABAs and Short-Acting Anticholinergics are used for acute symptom relief.
   - LABAs and LAMAs are the mainstays of maintenance therapy to prevent exacerbations and improve lung function.
   - Methylxanthines may be used as an adjunct therapy in certain cases, particularly when other bronchodilators are not providing adequate control.
3. **Other Conditions:** Bronchodilators may also be used in conditions such as bronchiectasis, cystic fibrosis, and other forms of obstructive lung diseases, where airway obstruction is a significant component.

Administration Techniques

Proper administration of bronchodilators is essential to ensure optimal drug delivery and therapeutic effect. The primary routes of administration

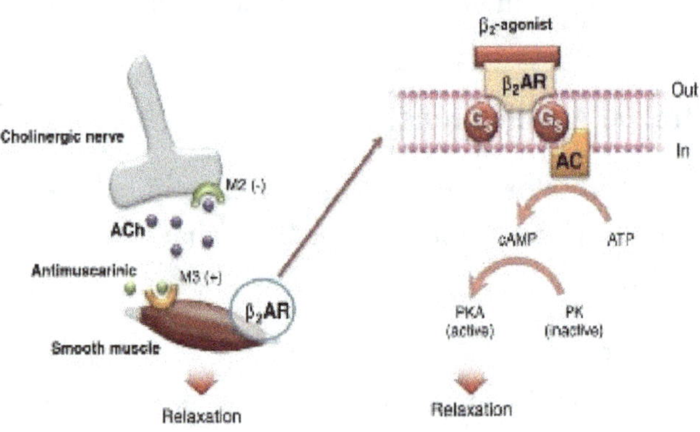

include inhalation, oral, and intravenous.

1. **Inhalation:** This is the preferred method for delivering bronchodilators, as it allows the medication to act directly on the lungs with minimal systemic absorption. Various devices are used for inhalation therapy:
   - **Metered-dose inhalers (MDIs)** are handheld devices that deliver a specific amount of medication in aerosol form. Using a spacer can improve drug delivery to the lungs.
   - **Dry Powder Inhalers (DPIs):** These devices deliver medication in a dry powder form and require a deep, forceful inhalation.
   - **Nebulizers:** These devices convert liquid medication into a fine mist, which is inhaled through a mouthpiece or mask. Nebulizers are particularly useful for patients who have difficulty using MDIs or DPIs.
2. **Oral:** Oral bronchodilators, such as theophylline, are used less frequently due to their systemic side effects and the need for blood level monitoring.
   - **Intravenous:** Intravenous administration is typically reserved for acute severe asthma or COPD exacerbations where a rapid onset of action is required. Drugs like aminophylline can be administered in this manner.

Monitoring and Safety

Monitoring the effectiveness and safety of bronchodilator therapy is crucial for achieving optimal outcomes and minimizing adverse effects.

1. **Efficacy:** Assessing the patient's symptom relief, lung function (via spirometry or peak flow measurements), and overall quality of life helps determine the effectiveness of the treatment regimen. Based on these assessments, adjustments may be needed.
2. **Side Effects:** Each class of bronchodilator has potential side effects that need to be monitored:
   - Beta-Agonists: Common side effects include tachycardia, palpitations, tremors, and, in some cases, hypokalemia. Excessive use can lead to tolerance and decreased efficacy.
   - Anticholinergics: Dry mouth, constipation, urinary retention, and, rarely, paradoxical bronchospasm are possible side effects.
   - Methylxanthines: Nausea, vomiting, headaches, and arrhythmias are notable side effects. Therapeutic drug monitoring is necessary to avoid toxicity.
3. **Patient Education:** Educating patients on the proper use of inhalers, recognizing signs of exacerbations, and the importance of adherence to the prescribed regimen is vital for effective disease management.

Emerging Therapies and Future Directions

Research and development in respiratory pharmacology continue to evolve, with the goal of improving the efficacy and safety of bronchodilator therapy. Some areas of interest include:

- **Novel Beta-Agonists:** Development of ultra-long-acting beta-agonists that provide prolonged bronchodilation with once-daily dosing.
- **Combination Inhalers:** Combining multiple classes of bronchodilators in a single inhaler to simplify treatment regimens and improve adherence.

- **Biologics:** Targeted therapies for specific inflammatory pathways involved in asthma and COPD, offering the potential for personalized medicine approaches.

DISCUSSION QUESTION

- Compare and contrast the mechanisms of action of beta-2 agonists, anticholinergics, and methylxanthines. How do these differences impact their clinical use?
- In what scenarios would combination therapy with bronchodilators be more beneficial than monotherapy, and what considerations must be made when prescribing combination therapy?

MODULE THREE

LESSON ONE: CORTICOSTEROIDS IN RESPIRATORY CARE

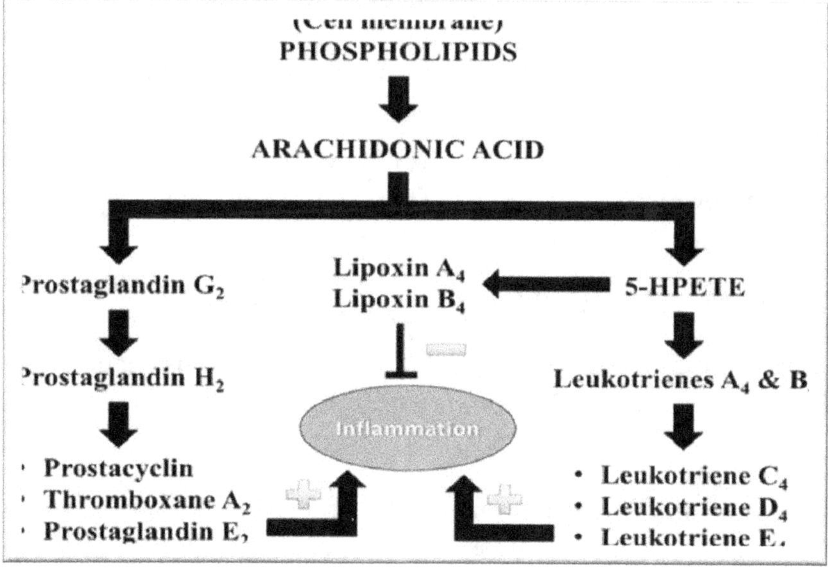

Corticosteroids are potent anti-inflammatory agents widely used in the treatment of various respiratory conditions, particularly asthma and chronic obstructive pulmonary disease (COPD). They play a critical role in controlling inflammation, reducing airway hyperresponsiveness, and preventing exacerbations. This lesson will explore the pharmacology of corticosteroids, their clinical applications, administration methods, and potential side effects.

Pharmacology of Corticosteroids

Corticosteroids are synthetic analogues of the natural hormone cortisol, produced by the adrenal cortex. They exert their effects by modulating the expression of various genes involved in inflammatory and immune responses.

- **Mechanism of Action:** Corticosteroids bind to glucocorticoid receptors in the cytoplasm, forming a receptor-steroid complex that translocates to the nucleus. There, it interacts with specific DNA sequences, known as glucocorticoid response elements (GREs), to regulate gene transcription. This results in the suppression of pro-inflammatory cytokines, chemokines, and other mediators, as well as the induction of anti-inflammatory proteins.
- **Anti-inflammatory Effects:** By inhibiting multiple inflammatory pathways, corticosteroids reduce the infiltration of inflammatory cells, decrease mucus production, and mitigate airway oedema. This leads to improved airflow and reduced symptoms in patients with asthma and COPD.

CLINICAL APPLICATIONS

Corticosteroids are used in various forms and regimens depending on the severity and type of respiratory condition:

1. **Asthma**
   - **Inhaled Corticosteroids (ICS)** are the cornerstone of asthma management for patients with persistent symptoms. Examples include fluticasone, budesonide, and beclomethasone. When used correctly, ICS are highly effective in reducing inflammation and preventing exacerbations with minimal systemic side effects.
   - **Systemic Corticosteroids:** Oral or intravenous corticosteroids, such as prednisone and methylprednisolone, are used for short-term management of acute severe asthma or exacerbations. Long-term use is generally avoided due to significant side effects.
2. **Chronic Obstructive Pulmonary Disease (COPD):**
   - Inhaled Corticosteroids: ICS are used in combination with long-acting bronchodilators for patients with severe COPD and frequent exacerbations. They help reduce the frequency and severity of exacerbations.

- Systemic Corticosteroids: Short courses of systemic corticosteroids are used during acute COPD exacerbations to reduce inflammation and improve symptoms.

3. **Other Conditions:** Corticosteroids may also be used in conditions such as interstitial lung diseases, allergic bronchopulmonary aspergillosis (ABPA), and severe pneumonia with significant inflammatory responses.

Administration Methods

The route of administration for corticosteroids depends on the desired effect and the clinical scenario:

- **Inhalation:** Inhaled corticosteroids are preferred for long-term management of asthma and COPD. They target the lungs directly, providing high local concentrations with minimal systemic exposure. Devices include metered-dose inhalers (MDIs), dry powder inhalers (DPIs), and nebulizers.
- **Oral:** Oral corticosteroids are used for short-term management of acute exacerbations in asthma and COPD. They are effective but carry a higher risk of systemic side effects with prolonged use.
- **Intravenous:** Intravenous corticosteroids are reserved for severe exacerbations or conditions where rapid and potent anti-inflammatory effect is required. Examples include methylprednisolone and hydrocortisone.

Dosing and Duration

The dosing and duration of corticosteroid therapy vary based on the condition being treated and the severity of symptoms. Key considerations include:

- **Inhaled Corticosteroids (ICS):** Dosages are typically categorized as low, medium, or high, depending on the specific drug and formulation. Treatment is usually long-term, with regular monitoring to adjust the dose as needed.

- **Systemic Corticosteroids:** For acute exacerbations, a short course (5-10 days) of oral or intravenous corticosteroids is commonly prescribed. Tapering off the dose may be necessary to prevent withdrawal symptoms and adrenal insufficiency, particularly after prolonged use.

Potential Side Effects

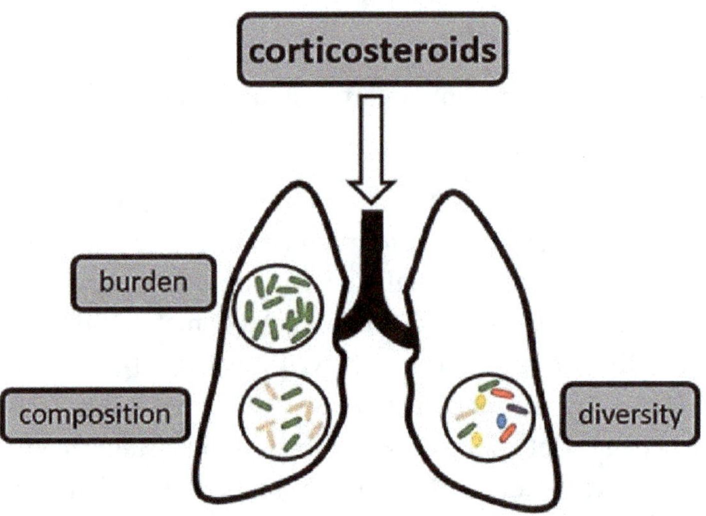

While corticosteroids are highly effective, they can also cause a range of side effects, particularly with long-term use. These side effects can be minimized by using the lowest effective dose and employing inhaled forms when possible.

1. **Inhaled Corticosteroids (ICS):**
   - Local Side Effects: These include oropharyngeal candidiasis (thrush), dysphonia (hoarseness), and cough. Using a spacer device with MDIs and rinsing the mouth after inhalation can reduce these effects.
   - Systemic Side Effects: Although less common, systemic absorption can occur, leading to potential side effects such as adrenal suppression, growth retardation in children, osteoporosis, and increased risk of pneumonia.

2. **Systemic Corticosteroids:**
   - Short-term Side Effects: Increased appetite, weight gain, mood changes, hyperglycemia, and hypertension.
   - Long-term Side Effects include osteoporosis, muscle weakness, cataracts, glaucoma, peptic ulcers, and increased susceptibility to infections. Chronic use can also lead to Cushing's syndrome, characterized by central obesity, moon face, and striae.

Monitoring and Management

Regular monitoring is essential to balance the benefits of corticosteroid therapy with the risk of side effects. Key aspects of monitoring include:

1. Efficacy: Assessing symptom control, lung function, frequency of exacerbations, and quality of life helps determine the effectiveness of therapy.
2. Side Effects: Monitoring for signs of systemic side effects, particularly with long-term use of systemic corticosteroids. Bone density scans, blood glucose levels, and eye examinations may be necessary.
3. Patient Education: Educating patients on the importance of adherence, proper inhaler technique, and strategies to minimize side effects is crucial for successful management.

Emerging Therapies and Future Directions

Research continues to explore new corticosteroid formulations and alternative anti-inflammatory treatments with the aim of improving efficacy and reducing side effects.

- **Inhaled Corticosteroids (ICS):** Development of ultra-fine particle formulations and combination inhalers that include ICS with long-acting bronchodilators or other anti-inflammatory agents.
- **Biologics:** Targeted therapies that modulate specific inflammatory pathways, such as interleukin-5 (IL-5)

inhibitors and interleukin-4/interleukin-13 (IL-4/IL-13) inhibitors, offering the potential for personalized treatment approaches.

- **Non-steroidal Anti-inflammatory Drugs (NSAIDs):** Ongoing research into new classes of anti-inflammatory drugs that could provide effective alternatives to corticosteroids.

DISCUSSION QUESTIONS

- Discuss the short-term and long-term side effects of corticosteroid use in respiratory care. How can healthcare providers balance the benefits and risks?
- How do inhaled corticosteroids compare to systemic corticosteroids in terms of efficacy and safety for treating respiratory conditions?

MODULE FOUR

LESSON ONE: ANTIBIOTICS FOR RESPIRATORY INFECTIONS

ANTIBIOTICS

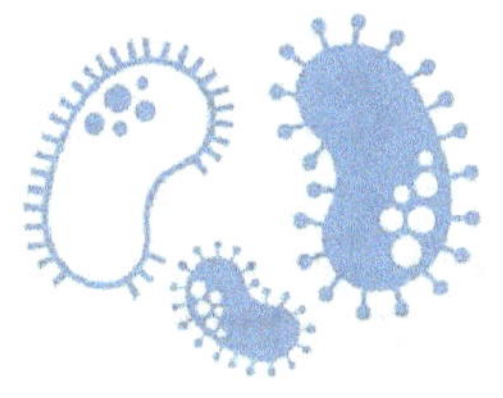

Does my child need antibiotics?
Antibiotics are only used to treat infections caused by **bacteria**, not infections caused by viruses, such as the common cold.

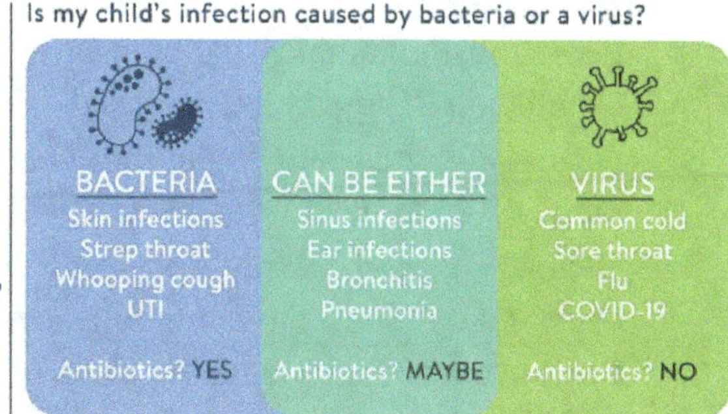

Antibiotics play a crucial role in the treatment of bacterial respiratory infections, which can range from mild conditions like bronchitis to severe illnesses such as pneumonia and tuberculosis. The appropriate use of antibiotics is essential to effectively eradicate infections, prevent complications, and mitigate the development of antibiotic resistance. In this lesson, we will explore the various classes of antibiotics used in respiratory care, their mechanisms of action, clinical applications, and guidelines for appropriate use.

Types of Respiratory Infections

Respiratory infections can be categorized based on their location within the respiratory tract:

- **Upper Respiratory Tract Infections (URTIs):** These include sinusitis, pharyngitis, and laryngitis. Most URTIs are viral, but bacterial infections can occur, necessitating antibiotic therapy.

- **Lower Respiratory Tract Infections (LRTIs):** These include bronchitis, pneumonia, and tuberculosis. Bacterial

LRTIs often require antibiotic treatment to prevent serious complications and ensure recovery.

Classes of Antibiotics

Several classes of antibiotics are commonly used to treat respiratory infections. Each class has a distinct mechanism of action and spectrum of activity:

1. **Beta-Lactams:**
   - Penicillins: Examples include amoxicillin and amoxicillin-clavulanate. They inhibit bacterial cell wall synthesis, leading to cell lysis and death. Penicillins are effective against a broad range of gram-positive and some gram-negative bacteria.
   - Cephalosporins: Examples include cefuroxime and ceftriaxone. Similar to penicillins, cephalosporins inhibit cell wall synthesis but have a broader spectrum of activity, including better coverage of gram-negative bacteria.
2. **Macrolides**: Examples include azithromycin and clarithromycin. These antibiotics inhibit bacterial protein synthesis by binding to the 50S ribosomal subunit. Macrolides are effective against a wide range of respiratory pathogens, including atypical bacteria like Mycoplasma pneumoniae and Chlamydia pneumoniae.
3. **Fluoroquinolones**: Examples include levofloxacin and moxifloxacin. They inhibit bacterial DNA gyrase and topoisomerase IV, preventing DNA replication and transcription. Fluoroquinolones have broad-spectrum activity, including coverage of gram-positive, gram-negative, and atypical bacteria.
4. **Tetracyclines**: Examples include doxycycline and tetracycline. These antibiotics inhibit protein synthesis by binding to the 30S ribosomal subunit. Tetracyclines are effective against a variety of respiratory pathogens, including atypical bacteria.
5. **Aminoglycosides**: Examples include gentamicin and tobramycin. They inhibit bacterial protein synthesis by binding to the 30S ribosomal subunit. Aminoglycosides are particularly effective against gram-negative bacteria but are often used in combination with other antibiotics due to their toxicity.

6. **Glycopeptides:** Examples include vancomycin. They inhibit cell wall synthesis by binding to the D-alanyl-D-alanine terminus of cell wall precursors. Glycopeptides are primarily used to treat gram-positive infections, including those caused by methicillin-resistant Staphylococcus aureus (MRSA).

Viruses or Bacteria
What's got you sick?

Antibiotics are often prescribed when they are not needed for respiratory infections. Antibiotics are only needed for treating certain respiratory infections caused by bacteria. Viral illnesses cannot be treated with antibiotics. When an antibiotic is not prescribed, ask your healthcare professional for tips on how to relieve symptoms and feel better.

5 things you should know about Antibiotics

Mechanisms of Action

Understanding the mechanisms of action of antibiotics is essential for selecting the appropriate drug and ensuring effective treatment:

- **Cell Wall Synthesis Inhibitors:** Beta-lactams and glycopeptides disrupt bacterial cell wall synthesis, leading to cell lysis and death. These antibiotics are particularly effective against actively dividing bacteria.
- **Protein Synthesis Inhibitors:** Macrolides, tetracyclines, and aminoglycosides interfere with bacterial protein synthesis by binding to ribosomal subunits. This prevents the production of essential proteins, inhibiting bacterial growth and replication.
- **DNA Synthesis Inhibitors:** Fluoroquinolones inhibit enzymes involved in DNA replication and transcription, preventing bacterial proliferation.

Clinical Applications

The choice of antibiotic depends on the type and severity of the respiratory infection, the suspected or confirmed pathogen, and patient-specific factors such as allergies and comorbidities:

- **Community-Acquired Pneumonia (CAP):** Empiric treatment often includes a macrolide (e.g., azithromycin) or a beta-lactam (e.g., amoxicillin) combined with a macrolide or doxycycline. Fluoroquinolones are used in patients with comorbidities or when atypical pathogens are suspected.
- **Hospital-Acquired Pneumonia (HAP) and Ventilator-Associated Pneumonia (VAP):** Treatment typically involves broader-spectrum antibiotics, such as piperacillin-tazobactam, cefepime, or a carbapenem, often combined with an aminoglycoside or vancomycin to cover MRSA.
- **Acute Exacerbations of Chronic Obstructive Pulmonary Disease (AECOPD):** Antibiotics like amoxicillin-clavulanate, doxycycline, or a macrolide are commonly used to treat bacterial exacerbations.
- **Tuberculosis:** A combination of antibiotics, including isoniazid, rifampin, ethambutol, and pyrazinamide, is used to treat tuberculosis due to the risk of resistance and the need for prolonged therapy.

Guidelines for Appropriate Use

Appropriate use of antibiotics is critical to ensure effective treatment and minimize the risk of antibiotic resistance:

- **Empiric Therapy:** Initial antibiotic selection is often empiric, based on the most likely pathogens and local resistance patterns. To guide definitive treatment, it is essential to obtain culture samples before starting empiric therapy.
- **Definitive Therapy:** Once culture results and antibiotic sensitivities are available, therapy should be adjusted to the most effective and narrow-spectrum antibiotic to target the identified pathogen.

- **Duration of Therapy:** The duration of antibiotic therapy should be based on clinical guidelines and the patient's response to treatment. Shorter courses of antibiotics are generally preferred to reduce the risk of resistance and side effects, provided they are effective.
- **Monitoring and Follow-Up:** Patients should be closely monitored for clinical improvement and potential side effects. In severe or persistent infections, follow-up cultures may be necessary to ensure the eradication of the pathogen.
- **Antibiotic Stewardship:** Healthcare providers should adhere to antibiotic stewardship principles, which include prescribing antibiotics only when necessary, using the appropriate drug, dose, and duration, and promoting preventive measures such as vaccination and infection control practices.

Potential Side Effects

Antibiotics, while essential for treating infections, can cause side effects that vary depending on the drug class and patient factors:

1. Beta-Lactams:
   - Penicillins: Allergic reactions ranging from rash to anaphylaxis, gastrointestinal disturbances, and, rarely, hematologic abnormalities.
   - Cephalosporins: Similar to penicillins, with a potential for cross-reactivity in patients with penicillin allergies.
2. **Macrolides:** Gastrointestinal side effects (nausea, vomiting, diarrhoea), QT interval prolongation leading to arrhythmias, and hepatotoxicity.
3. **Fluoroquinolones:** Tendonitis and tendon rupture, peripheral neuropathy, QT interval prolongation, and central nervous system effects such as confusion and seizures.
4. **Tetracyclines:** Gastrointestinal disturbances, photosensitivity, discolouration of teeth in children, and hepatotoxicity.
5. **Aminoglycosides:** Nephrotoxicity, ototoxicity (hearing loss), and neuromuscular blockade.

6. Glycopeptides: Nephrotoxicity, "red man syndrome" (a histamine release reaction), and, with prolonged use, ototoxicity.

Emerging Challenges and Future Directions

The emergence of antibiotic-resistant bacteria presents a significant challenge in the treatment of respiratory infections. Efforts to combat this issue include:

- Development of New Antibiotics: Research and development of novel antibiotics with unique mechanisms of action to overcome resistance.
- Rapid Diagnostic Tests: Advances in diagnostic technology to quickly identify pathogens and their resistance profiles, allowing for targeted therapy.
- Alternative Therapies: Investigating the use of bacteriophages, antimicrobial peptides, and other non-traditional therapies as potential treatments for resistant infections.
- Preventive Measures: Strengthening vaccination programs, improving infection control practices, and promoting public health initiatives to reduce the incidence of respiratory infections and the need for antibiotics.

DISCUSSION QUESTIONS

- What factors should be considered when selecting an antibiotic for treating a respiratory infection, and how can resistance patterns influence this choice?
- How can the overuse and misuse of antibiotics in respiratory infections be minimized to prevent antibiotic resistance?

MODULE FIVE

LESSON ONE: UNDERSTANDING INHALATION THERAPY

Inhalation therapy is a fundamental component of respiratory pharmacology, providing a direct route for delivering medications to the lungs, where they can exert their therapeutic effects with minimal systemic exposure. This lesson delves

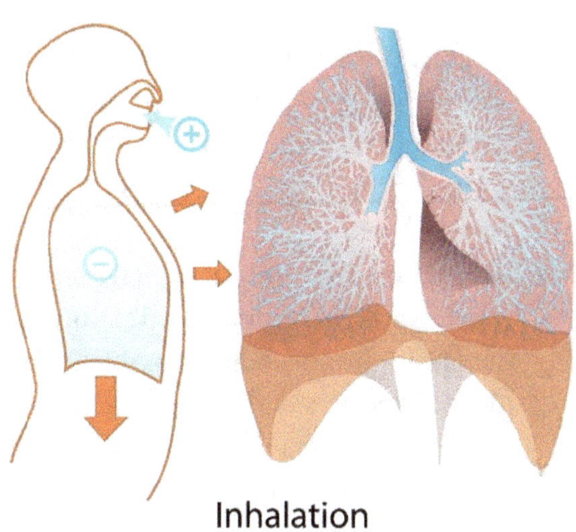

Inhalation

into the principles of inhalation therapy, the types of inhalation devices, the correct techniques for their use, and the benefits and challenges associated with inhalation therapy.

Principles of Inhalation Therapy

Inhalation therapy leverages the direct delivery of medications to the respiratory tract, offering several advantages:

- Localized Treatment: Medications are delivered directly to the site of action, enhancing their efficacy in treating respiratory conditions.
- Rapid Onset: Inhalation provides a quick onset of action, which is crucial for the relief of acute symptoms such as bronchospasm.

- Reduced Systemic Side Effects: By minimizing systemic absorption, inhalation therapy reduces the risk of side effects commonly associated with oral or intravenous medications.

Types of Inhalation Devices

There are several types of inhalation devices, each with specific features and benefits:

- **Metered-dose inhalers (MDIs):** These handheld devices deliver a specific amount of medication in aerosol form. Key components include a pressurized canister and a metering valve. MDIs require coordination between actuation and inhalation.
- **Dry Powder Inhalers (DPIs):** These devices deliver medication in a dry powder form and are breath-actuated, meaning the medication is released when the patient inhales deeply and forcefully. DPIs are easier to use for patients who struggle with the coordination required for MDIs.
- **Nebulizers:** Nebulizers convert liquid medication into a fine mist that can be inhaled through a mouthpiece or mask. They are particularly useful for patients who have difficulty using MDIs or DPIs, such as young children or those with severe respiratory conditions.
- **Soft Mist Inhalers (SMIs):** These devices produce a slow-moving mist, enhancing drug delivery to the lungs and reducing the need for precise coordination between actuation and inhalation.

Correct Techniques for Using Inhalation Devices

Proper technique is crucial to ensure the effective delivery of medication and optimal therapeutic outcomes. Key steps for using each type of inhalation device include:

1. **Metered-Dose Inhalers (MDIs):**
   - Shake the inhaler well before use.
   - Remove the cap and inspect the mouthpiece for any debris.

- Exhale fully to empty the lungs.
- Place the mouthpiece in the mouth, forming a tight seal with the lips.
- Press the canister to release the medication while simultaneously inhaling slowly and deeply.
- Hold the breath for 10 seconds, then exhale slowly.
- If a second dose is needed, wait at least 30 seconds before repeating the process.

2. **Dry Powder Inhalers (DPIs):**
   - Prepare the inhaler according to the manufacturer's instructions (e.g., loading a capsule or twisting the base).
   - Exhale fully away from the inhaler.
   - Place the mouthpiece in the mouth and inhale deeply and forcefully.
   - Hold the breath for 10 seconds, then exhale slowly.
   - Check the device to ensure the full dose was taken.

3. **Nebulizers:**
   - Assemble the nebulizer and add the prescribed medication to the medicine cup.
   - Attach the mouthpiece or mask and connect the nebulizer to the compressor.
   - Turn on the compressor to create the mist.
   - Breathe in the mist slowly and deeply until all the medication is used, usually taking 10-15 minutes.
   - Clean the nebulizer components according to the manufacturer's instructions after each use.

4. **Soft Mist Inhalers (SMIs):**
   - Prime the inhaler if it is the first use.
   - Exhale fully away from the inhaler.
   - Place the mouthpiece in the mouth and press the dose-release button while inhaling slowly and deeply.
   - Hold the breath for 10 seconds, then exhale slowly.

Benefits and Challenges of Inhalation Therapy

Benefits:

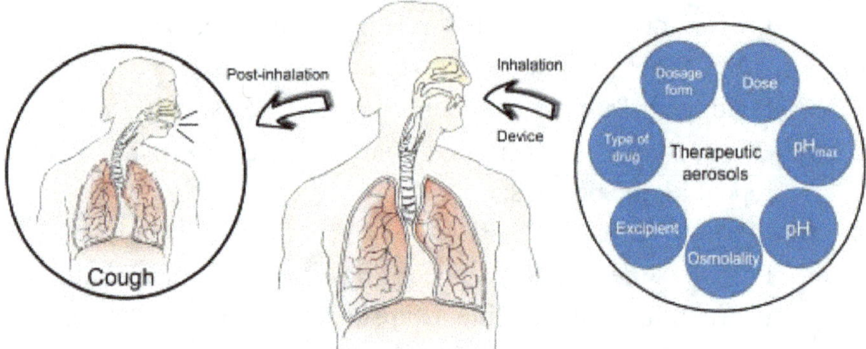

- Targeted Delivery: Medications reach the respiratory tract directly, providing effective relief with lower doses.
- Quick Onset: Inhalation therapy offers rapid relief of symptoms, which is especially important in acute conditions.
- Minimized Systemic Effects: Localized treatment reduces the likelihood of systemic side effects.

Challenges:

- Technique-Dependent: Effective use requires proper technique, which can be difficult for some patients, particularly the elderly or very young.
- Device Selection: Choosing the appropriate device for each patient can be challenging and requires consideration of patient preference, ability, and the specific medication.
- Maintenance and Cleanliness: Inhalation devices require regular cleaning and maintenance to prevent infections and ensure proper functioning.

Patient Education and Adherence

Educating patients on the correct use of inhalation devices is essential for effective therapy. Key points include:

- **Demonstration:** Healthcare providers should demonstrate the correct use of inhalers and nebulizers, allowing patients to practice under supervision.
- **Written Instructions:** Providing written instructions or instructional videos can reinforce proper technique.
- **Regular Review:** Periodically reviewing inhaler technique during follow-up visits helps ensure continued proper use.
- **Adherence**: Emphasizing the importance of adherence to prescribed therapy and addressing any barriers to adherence, such as cost or difficulty using the device, is crucial for optimal outcomes.

Future Directions

Advances in inhalation therapy continue to evolve, with ongoing research focused on improving drug formulations, inhaler design, and patient adherence:

- Smart Inhalers: Devices equipped with sensors and digital technology to monitor use, provide feedback, and enhance adherence.
- New Drug Formulations: Development of ultra-long-acting inhaled medications that reduce the frequency of dosing.
- Combination Inhalers: Inhalers that combine multiple medications to simplify treatment regimens and improve patient adherence.

DISCUSSION QUESTIONS

- What are the mechanisms by which mucolytics and expectorants improve airway clearance, and in which respiratory conditions are the most effective?
- Discuss the potential side effects and contraindications of mucolytics and expectorants. How can these be managed in clinical practice?

MODULE SIX

LESSON ONE: ANTI-INFLAMMATORY AGENTS AND IMMUNOMODULATORS

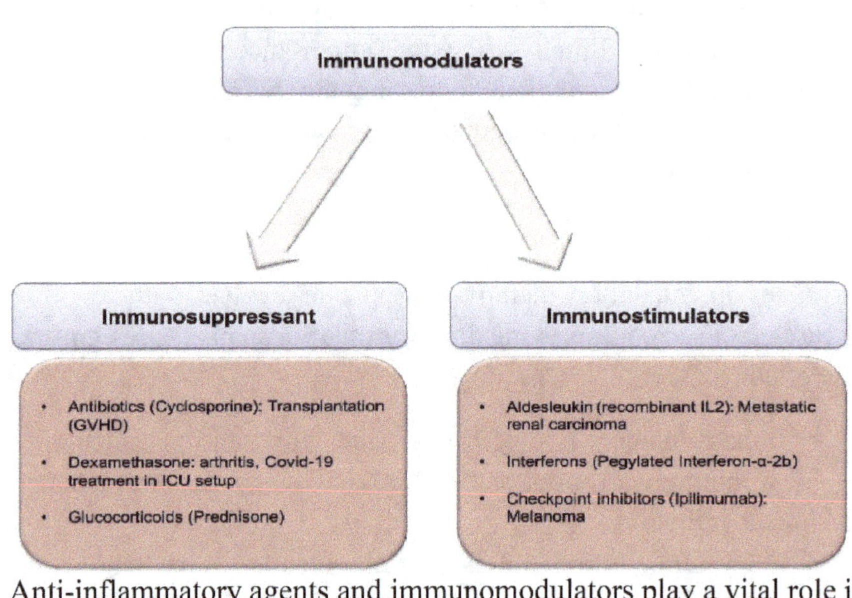

Anti-inflammatory agents and immunomodulators play a vital role in the management of respiratory diseases characterized by chronic inflammation and immune dysregulation, such as asthma, chronic obstructive pulmonary disease (COPD), and interstitial lung diseases. This lesson explores the different classes of anti-inflammatory agents and immunomodulators, their mechanisms of action, clinical applications, and considerations for their use in respiratory care.

CLASSES OF ANTI-INFLAMMATORY AGENTS

1. **Nonsteroidal Anti-inflammatory Drugs (NSAIDs):**
   - Mechanism of Action: NSAIDs inhibit cyclooxygenase (COX) enzymes, reducing the production of pro-inflammatory prostaglandins.
   - Clinical Applications: While NSAIDs are widely used for pain and inflammation in general, their use in respiratory

conditions is limited due to the risk of exacerbating asthma in some patients.

- Side Effects: Gastrointestinal disturbances, renal impairment, and increased risk of cardiovascular events.

2. **Corticosteroids:** Corticosteroids are potent anti-inflammatory agents used extensively in respiratory care.

- Mechanism of Action: They reduce inflammation by inhibiting multiple inflammatory pathways, including cytokine production and leukocyte migration.
- Clinical Applications: Used in asthma, COPD exacerbations, and interstitial lung diseases.
- Side Effects: Systemic side effects with long-term use, including osteoporosis, hyperglycemia, and adrenal suppression.

3. **Leukotriene Modifiers:**

- Mechanism of Action: These agents block leukotriene receptors or inhibit leukotriene synthesis, reducing inflammation and bronchoconstriction.
- Examples: Montelukast (leukotriene receptor antagonist) and zileuton (5-lipoxygenase inhibitor).
- Clinical Applications: Primarily used in asthma management, particularly in patients with allergic asthma or exercise-induced bronchoconstriction.
- Side Effects: Headache, gastrointestinal disturbances, and, rarely, neuropsychiatric events.

4. **Mast Cell Stabilizers:**

- Mechanism of Action: Prevent the release of inflammatory mediators from mast cells.
- Examples: Cromolyn sodium, nedocromil.
- Clinical Applications: Used as prophylactic therapy in asthma to prevent allergic reactions.
- Side Effects: Generally well-tolerated, with minimal side effects.

IMMUNOMODULATORS

1. **Biologics:**
   - **Mechanism of Action:** Biologics are targeted therapies that modulate specific components of the immune system.
   - **Examples:**
   ✓ Anti-IgE Antibodies: Omalizumab binds to immunoglobulin E (IgE) and prevents it from triggering allergic reactions. Used in severe allergic asthma.
   ✓ Anti-IL-5 Antibodies: Mepolizumab and reslizumab target interleukin-5 (IL-5), reducing eosinophilic inflammation. Used in severe eosinophilic asthma.
   ✓ Anti-IL-4/IL-13 Antibodies: Dupilumab inhibits interleukin-4 (IL-4) and interleukin-13 (IL-13) signaling. Used in moderate to severe asthma with an allergic component.
   - **Clinical Applications:** Biologics are used in patients with severe asthma who do not respond adequately to standard therapies.
   - **Side Effects:** Injection site reactions, increased risk of infections, and, rarely, anaphylaxis.
2. **Immunosuppressants:**
   - Mechanism of Action: These agents suppress the immune system to reduce inflammation and prevent tissue damage.
   - Examples: Methotrexate, azathioprine, mycophenolate mofetil, cyclosporine.
   - Clinical Applications: Used in interstitial lung diseases, such as sarcoidosis and idiopathic pulmonary fibrosis (IPF), and severe, refractory asthma.
   - Side Effects: Increased risk of infections, hepatotoxicity, nephrotoxicity, and bone marrow suppression.

Mechanisms of Action

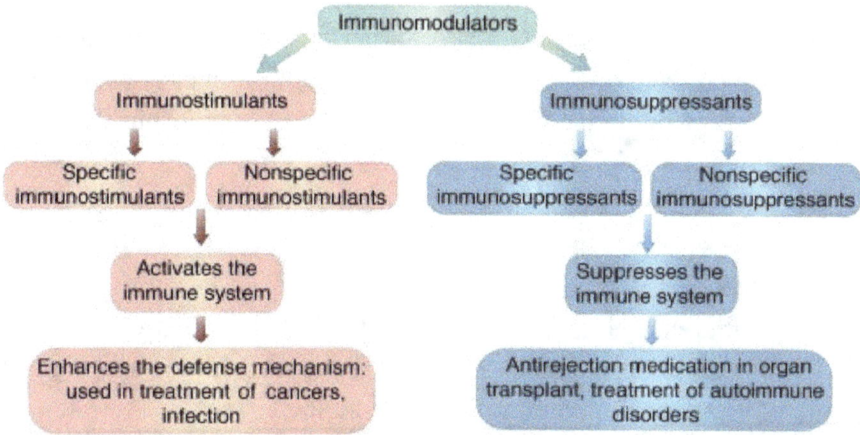

- Anti-inflammatory Agents: By reducing the production and activity of inflammatory mediators, these agents help to control chronic inflammation, reduce airway hyperresponsiveness, and prevent exacerbations.
- Immunomodulators: By targeting specific immune pathways, these agents modulate the immune response, reducing chronic inflammation and preventing tissue damage in respiratory diseases.

Clinical Applications

- **Asthma:** Anti-inflammatory agents, particularly inhaled corticosteroids and leukotriene modifiers, are mainstays in asthma management. Biologics are reserved for severe cases.
- **COPD:** Corticosteroids are used during exacerbations and in select patients with severe disease. Immunomodulators are less commonly used.
- **Interstitial Lung Diseases (ILDs):** Immunosuppressants are often used in the treatment of ILDs to reduce inflammation and prevent disease progression.
- **Allergic Conditions:** Anti-inflammatory agents, including mast cell stabilizers and leukotriene modifiers, are used to manage allergic respiratory conditions.

Considerations for Use

- Patient Selection: The appropriate agent is chosen based on the patient's specific respiratory condition, severity of disease, and patient-specific factors, such as comorbidities and potential side effects.
- Monitoring: Regular monitoring for efficacy and side effects is essential. This includes lung function tests, blood tests for systemic effects, and imaging studies for disease progression.
- Adherence: Ensuring patient adherence to therapy is critical for achieving optimal outcomes. Patient education and regular follow-up can help improve adherence.

Emerging Therapies and Future Directions

Research continues to explore new anti-inflammatory and immunomodulatory therapies to improve the management of respiratory diseases:

- Novel Biologics: The development of new biologics targeting different inflammatory pathways and immune cells offers the potential for more personalized and effective treatments.
- Small Molecule Inhibitors: Investigating small molecule inhibitors that target specific signalling pathways involved in inflammation and immune responses.
- Gene Therapy: Exploring the potential of gene therapy to correct genetic defects and modulate immune responses in certain respiratory diseases.

DISCUSSION QUESTIONS

- How do anti-inflammatory agents and immunomodulators differ in their approaches to managing chronic respiratory diseases, and what are their respective roles?
- What are the key considerations for monitoring patients on long-term anti-inflammatory or immunomodulatory therapy?

MODULE SEVEN

LESSON ONE: BRONCHODILATORS AND THEIR ROLE IN RESPIRATORY CARE

Bronchodilators are a cornerstone of respiratory pharmacology. They provide relief from

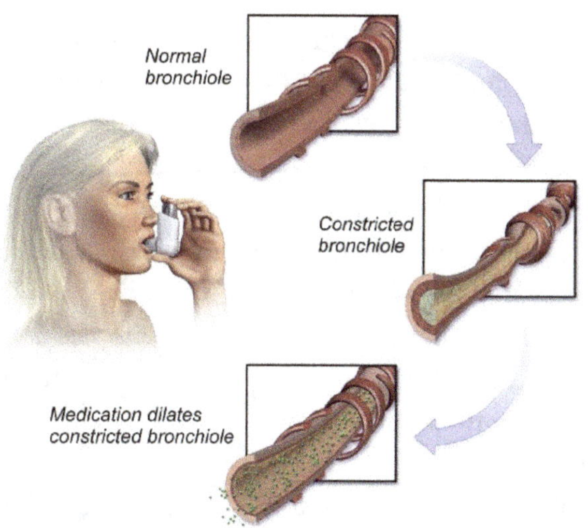

bronchoconstriction and improve airflow in conditions such as asthma and chronic obstructive pulmonary disease (COPD). This lesson delves into the different classes of bronchodilators, their mechanisms of action, clinical applications, and considerations for their use in respiratory care.

Classes of Bronchodilators

1. **Beta-2 Agonists:**
   - **Mechanism of Action:** Beta-2 agonists stimulate beta-2 adrenergic receptors in the smooth muscle of the airways, leading to muscle relaxation and bronchodilation.

- **Types:**
  - ✓ Short-Acting Beta-2 Agonists (SABAs): Examples include albuterol (salbutamol) and levalbuterol. These provide quick relief from acute bronchospasm.
  - ✓ Long-Acting Beta-2 Agonists (LABAs): Examples include salmeterol and formoterol. These provide prolonged bronchodilation and are used for maintenance therapy.

2. **Anticholinergics (Antimuscarinics):**
   - **Mechanism of Action:** Anticholinergics block muscarinic receptors in the smooth muscle of the airways, inhibiting the action of acetylcholine and leading to bronchodilation.
   - **Types:**
   - ✓ Short-Acting Anticholinergics: Examples include ipratropium. These provide relief from bronchospasm and are often used in combination with SABAs.
   - ✓ Long-Acting Anticholinergics (LAMAs): Examples include tiotropium and aclidinium. These provide prolonged bronchodilation for maintenance therapy.

3. **Methylxanthines:**
   - Mechanism of Action: Methylxanthines, such as theophylline, inhibit phosphodiesterase enzymes, leading to increased cyclic AMP levels and bronchodilation. They also have anti-inflammatory effects.
   - Clinical Applications: Used as an adjunct therapy in asthma and COPD, particularly in patients who do not respond adequately to inhaled bronchodilators.

Mechanisms of Action

Understanding the mechanisms of action of bronchodilators is essential for optimizing their use in respiratory care:

- Beta-2 Agonists: By stimulating beta-2 receptors, these agents cause smooth muscle relaxation and rapid bronchodilation, making them effective for both acute relief and maintenance therapy.

- Anticholinergics: By blocking muscarinic receptors, these agents reduce bronchoconstriction and mucus production, improving airflow and reducing symptoms.
- Methylxanthines: These agents cause bronchodilation and provide additional anti-inflammatory effects by increasing cyclic AMP levels, although a narrow therapeutic window and potential side effects limit their use.

CLINICAL APPLICATIONS

1. **Asthma:**
   - SABAs: Used as rescue inhalers for quick relief of acute bronchospasm.
   - LABAs: Used in combination with inhaled corticosteroids (ICS) for long-term control of asthma symptoms.
   - Methylxanthines: Used as an adjunct therapy in severe asthma.
2. **COPD:**
   - SABAs: Used for quick relief of acute symptoms and exacerbations.
   - LABAs and LAMAs: Used as maintenance therapy to reduce symptoms, improve lung function, and decrease exacerbations.
   - Methylxanthines: Used as an adjunct therapy in patients who do not respond adequately to inhaled bronchodilators.

Combination Therapy

Combination therapy often provides superior control of symptoms and better patient outcomes compared to monotherapy. Common combinations include:

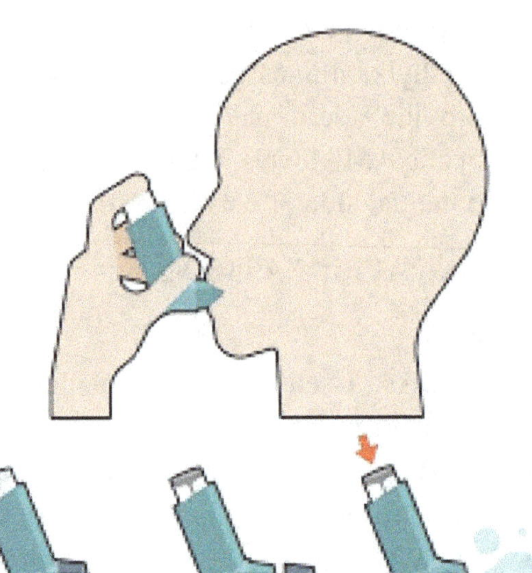

1. **LABA/ICS Combinations:**
   - Examples: 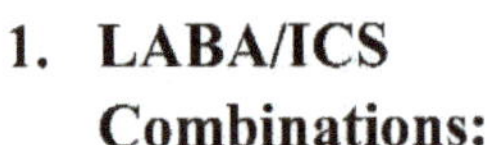

   Formoterol/budesonide, salmeterol/fluticasone.
   - Benefits: Provide both bronchodilation and anti-inflammatory effects, improving symptom control and reducing exacerbations in asthma.
2. **LABA/LAMA Combinations:**
   - Examples: Vilanterol/umeclidinium, formoterol/glycopyrrolate.
   - Benefits: Provide complementary bronchodilation through different mechanisms, improving lung function and reducing symptoms in COPD.
3. **Triple Therapy:**
   - Examples: LABA/LAMA/ICS combinations such as fluticasone/umeclidinium/vilanterol.
   - Benefits: Combining three agents provides maximal bronchodilation and anti-inflammatory effects, which is particularly beneficial in severe COPD.

Considerations for Use

When prescribing bronchodilators, healthcare providers must consider various factors to optimize treatment:

1. **Patient Assessment:** Evaluate the severity of the disease, frequency of symptoms, and patient-specific factors such as comorbidities and adherence potential.
2. **Side Effects:** Monitor for side effects specific to each class of bronchodilators:
   - Beta-2 Agonists: Tremor, tachycardia, and hypokalemia.
   - Anticholinergics: Dry mouth, urinary retention, and blurred vision.
   - Methylxanthines: Nausea, vomiting, insomnia, and cardiac arrhythmias.
3. **Inhaler Technique:** Educate patients on the correct use of inhalation devices to ensure effective drug delivery and therapeutic benefit.
4. **Regular Monitoring:** Periodically assess lung function, symptom control, and side effects to adjust therapy as needed.

Future Directions

Research in bronchodilator therapy is focused on developing new agents and improving existing treatments:

- **Novel Beta-2 Agonists:** Developing ultra-long-acting beta-2 agonists with a longer duration of action for once-daily dosing.
- **Next-Generation Anticholinergics:** Researching new anticholinergic agents with improved safety profiles and efficacy.
- **Combination Inhalers:** Continuing to develop and optimize combination inhalers that provide comprehensive management of respiratory diseases.
- **Personalized Medicine:** Using genetic and biomarker information to tailor bronchodilator therapy to individual patients for better outcomes.

DISCUSSION QUESTIONS

- How do the side effect profiles of different bronchodilators influence their use in specific patient populations?
- What are the advantages and disadvantages of using long-acting bronchodilators compared to short-acting bronchodilators in the management of chronic respiratory conditions?

MODULE EIGHT

LESSON ONE: CASE STUDIES AND CLINICAL APPLICATIONS

Applying the principles of respiratory pharmacology in real-world clinical scenarios is crucial for healthcare providers to

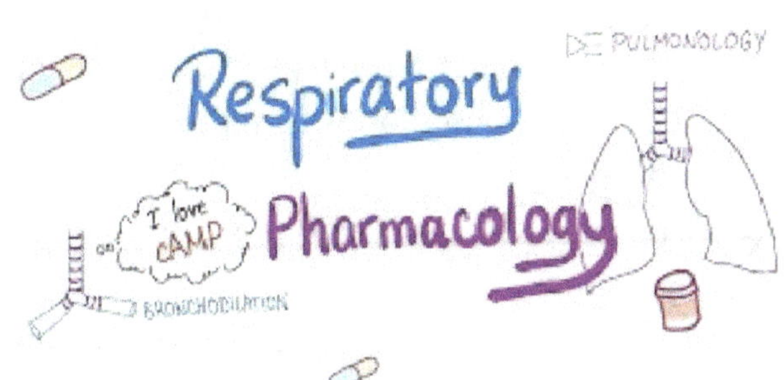

understand the practical aspects of managing respiratory diseases. This lesson presents various case studies to illustrate the application of knowledge gained from the previous module, highlighting the decision-making process, treatment strategies, and patient outcomes.

Case Study 1: Asthma Management in a Young Adult

Patient Profile:

- A 25-year-old male with a history of moderate persistent asthma.
- Symptoms include wheezing, shortness of breath, and cough, particularly at night and during exercise.
- Current medications: Albuterol inhaler (as needed).

Clinical Presentation:

- The patient reports increased use of the albuterol inhaler, with symptoms occurring three times a week and nighttime awakenings twice a month.

Assessment:

- Spirometry shows an FEV1 of 70% predicted, with significant improvement post-bronchodilator.
- The Asthma Control Test (ACT) score indicates suboptimal control.

Treatment Plan:

- Initiate Inhaled Corticosteroid (ICS): Prescribe a low-dose ICS (e.g., fluticasone) to reduce inflammation and improve control.
- Continue Albuterol: Continue as a rescue inhaler for acute symptoms.
- Education: Provide education on asthma triggers, correct inhaler technique, and the importance of adherence to ICS therapy.
- Follow-Up: Schedule a follow-up visit in 4-6 weeks to reassess control and adjust therapy if needed.

Outcome:

- At follow-up, the patient reports fewer symptoms, improved ACT score, and better overall control.
- Spirometry shows improved FEV1, indicating effective management with the addition of ICS.

Case Study 2: COPD Management in an Elderly Patient

Patient Profile:

- A 68-year-old female with a 30-pack-year smoking history and diagnosed with moderate COPD.
- Symptoms include chronic cough, sputum production, and dyspnea on exertion.
- Current medications: None.

Clinical Presentation:

- The patient reports increased breathlessness and difficulty performing daily activities.
- Physical examination reveals wheezing and decreased breath sounds.

Assessment:

- Spirometry confirms COPD with an FEV1/FVC ratio of 60% and FEV1 of 50% predicted.
- The Modified Medical Research Council (mMRC) Dyspnea Scale score indicates moderate dyspnea.

Treatment Plan:

- Initiate Long-Acting Bronchodilator: Prescribe a LABA (e.g., salmeterol) to improve airflow and reduce symptoms.
- Consider LAMA: Add a LAMA (e.g., tiotropium) for enhanced bronchodilation and symptom control.
- Smoking Cessation: Provide support and resources for smoking cessation, including counseling and nicotine replacement therapy.
- Pulmonary Rehabilitation: Refer to a pulmonary rehabilitation program to improve physical function and quality of life.
- Follow-Up: Schedule a follow-up visit in 4-6 weeks to reassess symptoms and lung function.

Outcome:

- At follow-up, the patient reports improved dyspnea, increased exercise tolerance, and reduced cough.
- Spirometry shows stabilization of lung function, indicating effective management with the combination of LABA and LAMA.

Case Study 3: Management of Community-Acquired Pneumonia (CAP)

Patient Profile:

- A 45-year-old male with no significant past medical history.
- Symptoms include fever, productive cough, and pleuritic chest pain for the past three days.

Clinical Presentation:

- Physical examination reveals crackles in the right lower lobe.
- Chest X-ray confirms right lower lobe consolidation.

Assessment:

- Diagnosis of community-acquired pneumonia (CAP) based on clinical presentation and imaging.

Treatment Plan:

- Empiric Antibiotic Therapy: Initiate empiric antibiotic therapy with a macrolide (e.g., azithromycin) or a beta-lactam (e.g., amoxicillin) plus a macrolide.
- Supportive Care: Recommend rest, hydration, and over-the-counter medications for symptom relief.
- Follow-Up: Advise follow-up in 48-72 hours to assess response to treatment and adjust antibiotics if needed based on clinical response and culture results.

Outcome:

- At follow-up, the patient reports resolution of fever, decreased cough, and improved overall condition.
- Repeat chest X-ray shows clearing of consolidation, indicating successful treatment of CAP.

DISCUSSION QUESTIONS

- How can case studies enhance the understanding and application of respiratory pharmacology in clinical practice?
- Discuss the importance of personalized treatment plans in respiratory care. How can healthcare providers ensure that treatments are tailored to individual patient needs?

CONCLUSION

Respiratory pharmacology plays a pivotal role in the effective management of various respiratory conditions, from asthma and chronic obstructive pulmonary disease (COPD) to respiratory infections and interstitial lung diseases. A thorough understanding of the mechanisms of action, clinical applications, and potential side effects of respiratory medications enables healthcare providers to tailor treatments to individual patient needs, ultimately improving patient outcomes and quality of life.

Throughout this comprehensive guide, we have explored the different classes of respiratory medications, including bronchodilators, corticosteroids, antibiotics, mucolytics, expectorants, anti-inflammatory agents, and immunomodulators. Each module delved into the pharmacological principles underlying these medications, their therapeutic uses, and the considerations necessary for their safe and effective administration.

Respiratory pharmacology is a dynamic and essential aspect of healthcare that requires a deep understanding of both fundamental principles and practical applications. By mastering these concepts and staying abreast of ongoing developments, healthcare providers can significantly improve the lives of individuals suffering from respiratory conditions, leading to better health outcomes and enhanced quality of life for their patients.

REFERENCES

- Barnes, P. J. (2010). *"Mechanisms of action of glucocorticoids in asthma."* American Journal of Respiratory and Critical Care Medicine.
- Barnes, P. J. (2011). *"Biochemical basis of asthma."* Annual Review of Biochemistry.
- Barnes, P. J. (2013). *"The pharmacology of bronchodilators."* Pharmacological Reviews, 65(4), 1135-1170.
- Boulet, L. P., & Boulay, M. È. (2015). *"Asthma-related comorbidities."* Expert Review of Respiratory Medicine.
- Cazzola, M., Matera, M. G., & Lötvall, J. (2005). *"Leukotriene modifiers in the treatment of asthma: An update."* Current Opinion in Pulmonary Medicine.
- GINA (Global Initiative for Asthma). (2021). *"Global Strategy for Asthma Management and Prevention."*
- GOLD (Global Initiative for Chronic Obstructive Lung Disease). (2021). *"Global Strategy for the Diagnosis, Management, and Prevention of Chronic Obstructive Pulmonary Disease."*
- Hogg, J. C., & Timens, W. (2009). "The pathology of chronic obstructive pulmonary disease." Annual Review of Pathology: Mechanisms of Disease.
- Jackson, D. J., & Johnston, S. L. (2010). *"The role of viruses in acute exacerbations of asthma."* The Journal of Allergy and Clinical Immunology.
- Pauwels, R. A., Buist, A. S., Calverley, P. M., Jenkins, C. R., & Hurd, S. S. (2001). *"Global strategy for the diagnosis, management, and prevention of chronic obstructive pulmonary disease."* American Journal of Respiratory and Critical Care Medicine.